BABY SEALS

By Katie Kawa

Gareth Stevens
Publishing

Please visit our website, www.garethstevens.com. For a free color catalog of all our high-quality books, call toll free 1-800-542-2595 or fax 1-877-542-2596.

Library of Congress Cataloging-in-Publication Data

Kawa, Katie.
Baby seals / Katie Kawa.
    p. cm.— (Cute and cuddly–baby animals)
ISBN 978-1-4339-5536-5 (pbk.)
ISBN 978-1-4339-5537-2 (6-pack)
ISBN 978-1-4339-5534-1 (library binding)
1. Seals (Animals)—Infancy—Juvenile literature. I. Title.
QL737.P64K39 2011
599.79'139—dc22

                                    2010052582

First Edition

Published in 2012 by
Gareth Stevens Publishing
111 East 14th Street, Suite 349
New York, NY 10003

Copyright © 2012 Gareth Stevens Publishing

Editor: Katie Kawa
Designer: Andrea Davison-Bartolotta

Photo credits: Cover, pp. 1, 5, 7, 11, 13, 15, 17, 19, 21, 24 (all) Shutterstock.com; p. 9 Joel Sartore/National Geographic/Getty Images; p. 23 Frank Greenaway/Dorling Kindersley/Getty Images.

Printed in the United States of America

CPSIA compliance information: Batch #CS11GS: For further information contact Gareth Stevens, New York, New York at 1-800-542-2595.

Contents

Baby seals are called pups.

A mother seal is called a cow.

Mother seals have one
baby every year.

Baby seals are born
on land.

A baby seal drinks milk. The milk makes it grow fast!

Then, baby seals go in the water. They learn to swim.

Baby seals have four flippers. These help them swim.

A baby seal has long hairs on its face. These help it find food.

Baby seals eat fish.

21

Baby seals sleep under the water.

Words to Know

flippers

hairs

Index